SCHIRMER'S LIBRARY
OF MUSICAL CLASSICS

T0066202

Vol. 2151

BEETHOVEN
SELECTED PIANO PIECES

FOR EARLY ADVANCED LEVEL

10 Selections from
Sonatas, Sonatinas, Variations and more

ISBN 978-1-5400-8986-1

G. SCHIRMER, Inc.

DISTRIBUTED BY

7777 W. BLUEMOUND RD. P.O. BOX 13819 MILWAUKEE, WI 53213

Visit Hal Leonard Online at
www.halleonard.com

Contact us:
Hal Leonard
7777 West Bluemound Road
Milwaukee, WI 53213
Email: info@halleonard.com

In Europe, contact:
Hal Leonard Europe Limited
42 Wigmore Street
Marylebone, London, W1U 2RN
Email: info@halleonardeurope.com

In Australia, contact:
Hal Leonard Australia Pty. Ltd.
4 Lentara Court
Cheltenham, Victoria, 3192 Australia
Email: info@halleonard.com.au

CONTENTS

ANDANTE
in F Major
"Andante Favori"

Ludwig van Beethoven
WoO 57

Andante grazioso con moto

to Count Franz von Brunsvik

FANTASIE
in G minor

Ludwig van Beethoven
Op. 77

*Fingering by Beethoven.

Allegretto

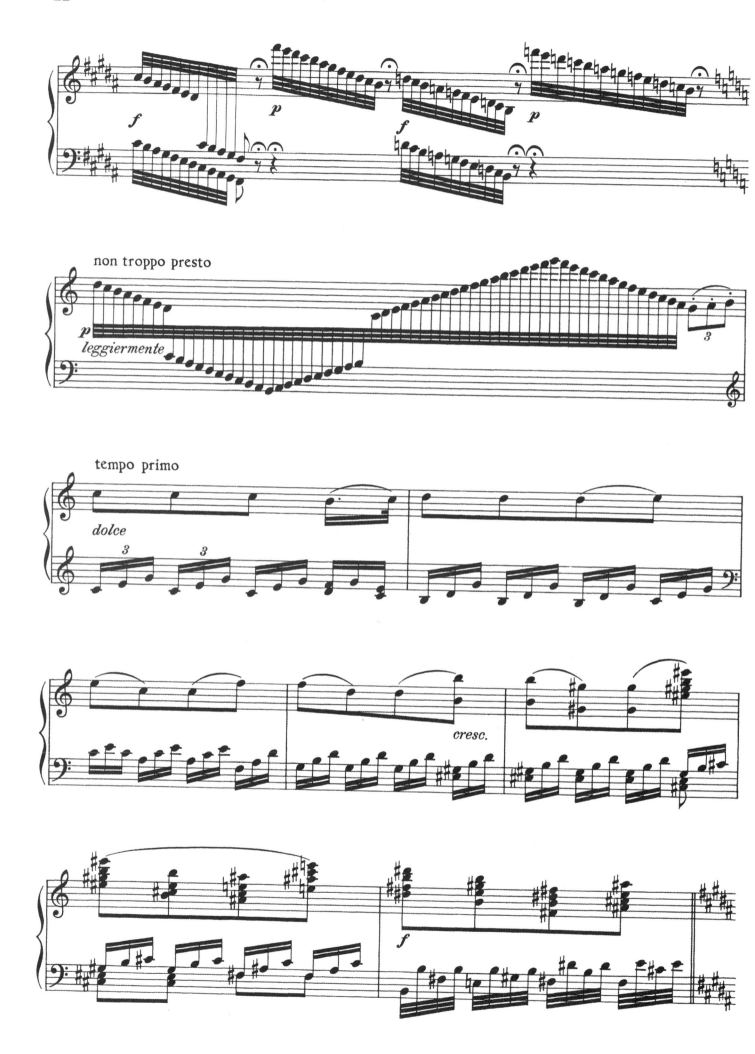

to Empress Elisabeth Alexievna of Russia

POLONAISE
in C Major

Ludwig van Beethoven
Op. 89

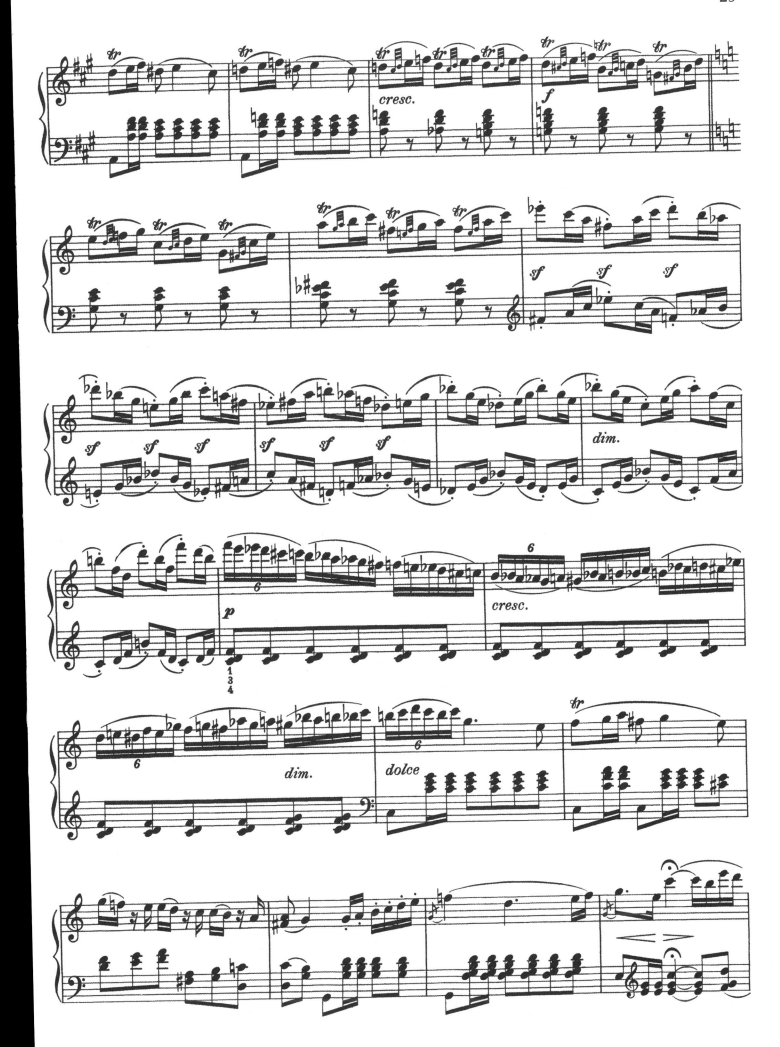

RONDO A CAPRICCIO

in Hungarian Style
"Rage Over a Lost Penny"

Ludwig van Beethoven
Op. 129

a) The opus number given to this piece, 129, seems to place it among the incomparable late works of Beethoven, written in the 1820's, the final years of the composer's life: the *Diabelli Variations, Missa Solemnis, Ninth Symphony,* Late Quartets, and the *Grosse Fuge.* But, this boisterous and exuberant character piece, molded into a strict classical *Rondo,* was not the work of a mature, visionary, experimental tone poet, but of a boldly emerging young composer. It is the music of a Beethoven full of youthful abandon, perhaps even wildness, eager to gain and please a public and stake out a career, rather than the Beethoven of 30 years later, the transcendental Master, abstract thinker, and musical visionary. Accord-ing to *Grove's Dictionary of Music and Musicians,* the piece was composed in 1795, and not published until 1828, one year following Beethoven's death. At that time, it was considered minor Beethoven, certainly not worthy of the composer of the *Fifth Symphony* and the *Emperor Concerto.* The fanciful subtitle, "Rage Over A Lost Penny" was added by the publisher, not by the composer, undoubtedly to boost sales by capitalizing on the late composer's great fame. Now, we can play it and hear it as an example of the stunning, vigorous public Beethoven, bedazzling an audience with his ferocious pianism and compositional brilliance.

The melodic thread (i.e., the rhythmic phrasing) ought to be brought out with extreme clarity;

Dedicated to the Princely Archbishop of Cologne, Maximilian Friedrich

SONATINA
in F minor

Ludwig van Beethoven
WoO 47, No. 2

Larghetto maestoso

Allegro assai

Allegro assai

To Princess Odeschalchi

SIX VARIATIONS
On an Original Theme

Edited and fingered by
Sigmund Lebert

Ludwig van Beethoven
Op. 34

Tema.

(a) Duly emphasize the melody throughout.
(b) Begin and end these arpeggios simultaneously in both hands, and play *crescendo* from the lowest to the highest tones, so that only the latter attain the power demanded by the signs *sf*, *mf* (further on, *f*.)

(c) Strike the first note of the arpeggio-figure together with the *f* in the bass.

(d)

(e)

N.B. All expression-marks in *small* type, both in this and all succeeding numbers, were added by the Editor. [Translator's Note.]

Var. I.

Var. II.

Allegro, ma non troppo. (♩. = 69)

(a) To be played throughout the measure *forte*, without *decrescendo*, so that the subsequent *piano* may surprise by its abrupt entrance.

58

Allegretto. (♩ = 120)

Var. III.

(a) (b) Carefully observe the abrupt *piano*.

Marcia. (a)
Allegretto. (♪=80.)

Var.V.

(a) This is, of course, a dead-march, and should, therefore, be played with solemn pathos, despite the *"allegretto"* tempo, which, moreover, ought to be taken very slowly.

Var. VI.

Allegretto. (♩.=54.)

The fermata may, as here indicated, be lengthened to fill out a whole measure, so that the trill ends on the third eighth-note of its third measure, with a very short lifting of the after-beat, together with which the left hand and the pedal are to be raised.

(a) Beware of accentuating the right-hand part as if *three* sixteenth-notes belonged to one beat.

The four final quarter-notes must each have nearly the time-value of an eighth-note in the following *"Adagio molto,"* and lead directly into the latter, so that the *c* before the $\frac{2}{4}$ time appears as the *auftakt* of the theme.

(d) The 128th-notes should be played, as far as distinctness allows, in tempo.

(f) Bring out the melody in the tenor.

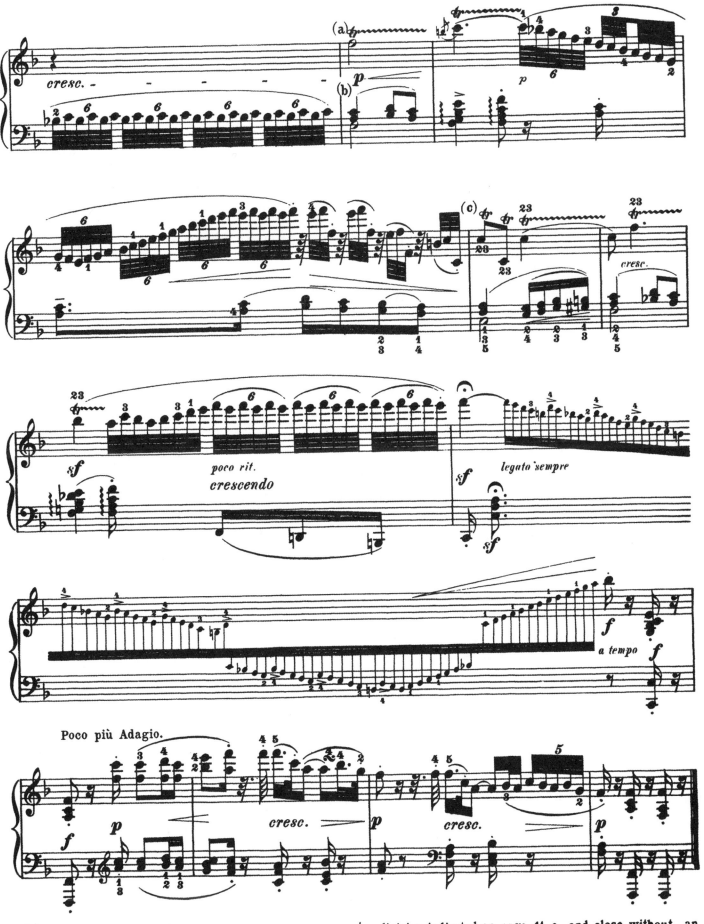

(a) Trill as on page 10, e.
(b) Bring out the melody in the tenor.
(c) Begin all these trills on the principal note, with the division indicated on page 41, e, and close without an after-beat; (at the last of these trills, it is also better to omit the after-beat).

NINE VARIATIONS
on a March by Dressler

Ludwig van Beethoven
WoO 63

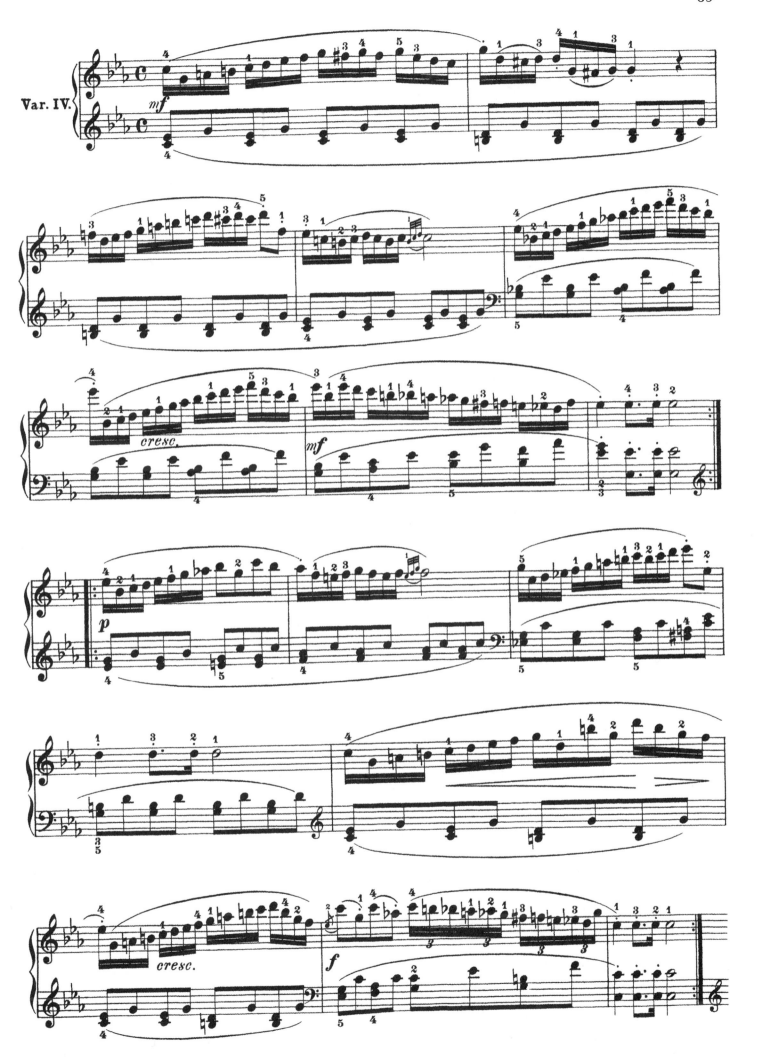

BAGATELLE

in C Major

Ludwig van Beethoven
Op. 33, No. 5

BAGATELLE
in B minor

Ludwig van Beethoven
Op. 126, No. 4

Presto

Dedicated to Countess Julie Guicciardi

SONATA
in C-sharp minor
(Quasi una Fantasia) "Moonlight"

Edited by Carl Krebs

Ludwig van Beethoven
Op. 27, No. 2

Adagio sostenuto.
Si deve suonare tutto questo pezzo delicatissimamente e senza sordino.

cresc.

p

cresc.

p

ppp

decresc.

pp

pp
attacca subito
il seguente.

Allegretto.
La prima parte senza repetizione.

Trio.

Presto agitato.

Allegretto da capo.

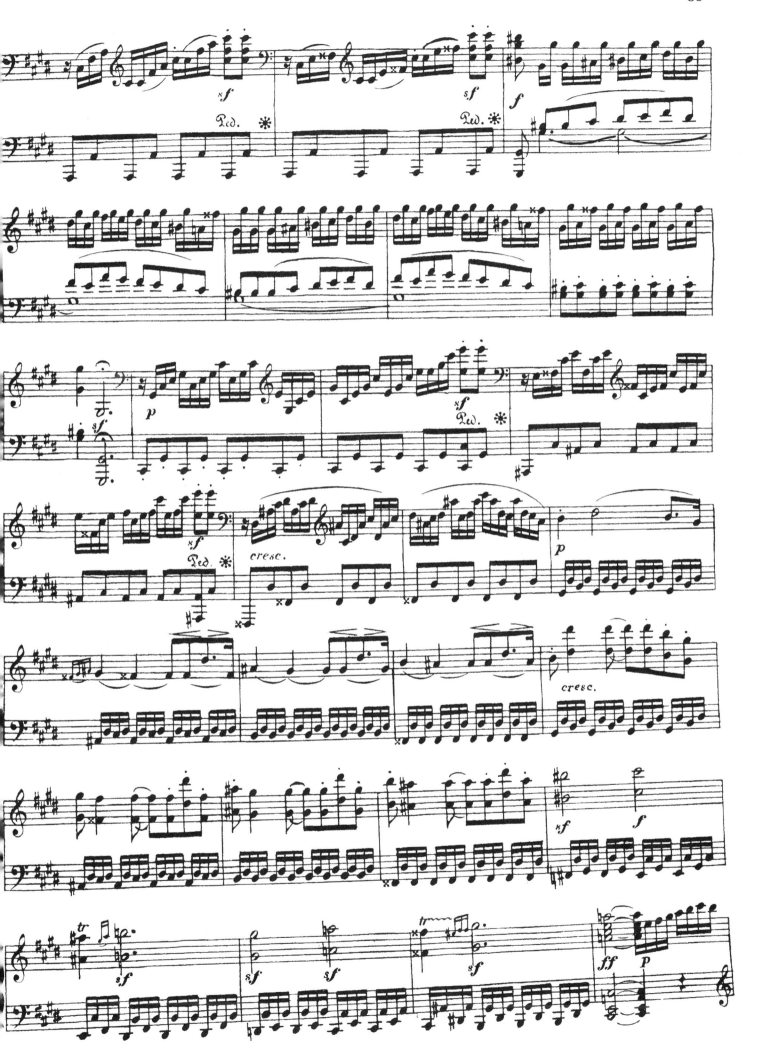

Adagio. **Tempo I.**

CLASSIC
ROCK SONGS
— IN A —
CLASSICAL
STYLE

Arranged by David Pearl

ISBN 978-1-70514-210-3

Visit Hal Leonard Online at
www.halleonard.com

Contact us:
Hal Leonard
7777 West Bluemound Road
Milwaukee, WI 53213
Email: info@halleonard.com

In Europe, contact:
Hal Leonard Europe Limited
42 Wigmore Street
Marylebone, London, W1U 2RN
Email: info@halleonardeurope.com

In Australia, contact:
Hal Leonard Australia Pty. Ltd.
4 Lentara Court
Cheltenham, Victoria, 3192 Australia
Email: info@halleonard.com.au